Theologies of Terrain

Tim Conroy

Theologies of Terrain

Tim Conroy

edited by

Ed Madden

Poet Laureate
Columbia, South Carolina

The Laureate Series

THEOLOGIES OF TERRAIN

Library of Congress Number: 2017955413
ISBN: 978-1-942081-14-2

Cover Photo by Kathleen Robbins

Theologies of Terrain by Tim Conroy is the first book in The Laureate Series, an endeavor of Muddy Ford Press to celebrate the tradition of poetry that is born to South Carolinians, and to promote and honor the relationship between Mentor and Protégé, Advocate and Postulant, Poet and Poet.

The Laureate Series

The Laureate Series

To certain people there comes a day
when they must say the great Yes or the great No.
He who has the Yes ready within him reveals him-
self at once, and saying it he crosses over

to the path of honor and his own conviction.
He who refuses does not repent. Should he be
asked again, he would say No again. And yet
that— No the right No— crushes him for the rest
of his life.

C. P. Cavafy, "Che Fece … Il Gran Refiuto

Send your second soul beyond the mountains,
beyond time.
Tell me what you saw, I will wait.

Czeslaw Milosz

Dedication

This work is dedicated to my courageous wife and best friend, Terrye McKenzie Conroy.

To Phillip, Lindsay, and Jackson and the magic that surrounds team Weathers.

To Jerrye McElwee—I can still hear your voice.

Contents

Introduction

Tim Conroy is a theologian of the best kind, a theologian of the ordinary. He knows, as we learn from the rough father in the first poem, that there are no assurances in this life—and there probably isn't another. We face crushing loss and daily difficulties. We have to learn to live the best we can here, now.

For Conroy, truth won't be found in the pews. It will be found in the small blessings of daily coffee in a familiar cafe, or the careful act of rubbing lotion on an old woman's skin, not forgetting the dry spot by her nose. No wonder that there is an ode to a mender here, to one who would mend what is torn, gather and fold what is scattered and tossed, and there are poems for many kinds of caregivers (most of them women), imperfect or ineffective though they may sometimes be.

There are two cathedrals in this book. One is "a cathedral of glances" where someone's always clutching a "pocketbook of judgment." The other is the natural world. "Enter the biome, / wind-swept pilgrim," Conroy writes in "Whispers of Trees," surely a concise revision of Robert Frost's "Directive." Conroy points us to a "cathedral" of trees where we are encouraged to find not truth or healing but perspective—to measure ourselves "by how a towering / moment passes." There's something deeply sacramental here, so it's not surprising that the poem ends with a command that we "absorb the wafer" of this moment. Conroy is part of a long tradition in American poetry, the visionary poet of the ordinary and natural world.

As he says near the end of the book, "I have felt a voice / in the forest of owls and ordinary spaces."

In "Theology of Terrain," Conroy is sure that there is some promise "deep in this land," He wants to find spiritual meaning in the natural world, and he insists that it offers healing and solace, or at least the potential for these things. But the natural world is always overwritten by the human. The horizon is inscribed by memory—especially memories of fathers and brothers. Some of these memories are difficult, he admits, but he urges us to stick with them, to find the truth in them. He also recognizes that the natural world is threatened by the human—not just the critters who learn "the perils of living / with creatures like us" in "Motion Detectors," but the wild geese in "Conventional Wisdom," who (pace Mary

Oliver) aren't headed home but are confused by climate change and shitting on our cars.

And we are ourselves imperfect and mortal. While this is obvious, Conroy reminds not to love our neighbor, but to remember "your neighbor is human." Remember that we are all sometimes rescued by strangers, all sometimes saved by love.

There are so many lovely things in this book. There are poems that break me and poems that resonate long after I've turned the page. I am delighted to help bring this beautiful book into the world.

This is a book not of answers but of questions. The book opens asking: will we be all right? Maybe. Maybe not. As Conroy says in one of the best poems in this book, "Marsh Deer," "Lives are as fleeting as bird songs, / as long as letting go." Maybe "will we be all right" is not the right question. Conroy leads us toward the better questions that end this book, not questions about our own survival, but questions about our relationships with one another.

Ed Madden
Poet Laureate
Columbia, South Carolina

I

Assurances

It comes to this:
Will we be all right?
A son needs a father
to answer. For a few years
after the Colonel retired
from the Marine Corps,
he worked as a Pinkerton
security cop in Atlanta.
During my visits from college,
he would drag me along
with him on third shift.
We would cruise by
landing strips of warehouses
into the horizon between
us. In a loop-the-loop
maneuver, he would peer out
from a Ford LTD's window
with an aviator's keen eye
looking for an enemy
from the night sky
emerging from a bank
of metal buildings
accelerating in North Korea
or from skies over Nam
with one hand at 12 o'clock.
If he spotted a door ajar,
he would hand me
the flashlight and bark

Check it out jocko.
I would moan, half asleep
and alert to the danger,
hop out entering darkness
ready to love him with light
shaking, exploring impenetrable
places to check for what might
still be there. I might
spot men sleeping,
smell cheap liquor—
probably former Pinkertons
or Marines I thought.
I'd close doors, report
that it was all clear.

My father would call me
a good pussy, then say,
There're no assurances in this life.

Two Little Joes

I stay at the edge of my bed to recall
a toothy baby brother. The tracks shudder
as a horn blasts warnings, disturbing
the city's sleep. Memories vibrate closer but
rumble away too soon. The train's blasts
were among the last sounds he heard.

As youngsters, in Pensacola, Tommy and I
slept in the same bed. We conspired a game
timed to a mother's shuffling slippers and soft
voice waking us for school. We'd wink, two
Little Joes galloping on calicos across the
Ponderosa, cutting into the back of a teepee
on a daring rescue mission. Then we'd make
the bed still in it, grip the sheet and bedspread
taut in a high arc overhead, arms stretched,
giggling, and fall

on opposite sides in unison to create a
smooth surface. He was dead at 33—a
suicidal leap before dawn. How do you derail
crushing loss? When you hear a horn blast,
pray it never stops. Listen at the edge of the
bed.

Journey

Feet blistered,
boots frozen, socks wet,

treacherous root and rock,
you stretch for a foothold,

fret about the weather,
shouldering essentials.

Miles beyond exhaustion,
ascending and descending,

you break; toughen, break again,
flat is a miracle.

You calculate the time
between doubt and town.

On this journey you inventory
all it is you carry.

A Wrath of Verses

The boy hears 10,000 men are slaughtered,
by blade to blood to body dung,
cedars burning, an ear near a lily. He
forgets his turn to read. A book
whacks his head in repudiation.
Deep into regret, his father dips a
hand in the toilet tank and retrieves
the bottle of Seagram's. Kneels in a
dwelling of black and white, prays to
a better Father, swigs, recalls his begetter,
stern palms that never touched cheeks,
two fingers still stuck against ribs,
a wrath of verses.

Craving dreams, the boy tosses to a hot
breakfast when his mom was around
to cook pancakes, sausage, and eggs
with a sizzling of love. He smells joy
but knows what awaits is the cold cereal
of proverbs; to make him feel not chosen,
to make him not care who he slays.
Last week, he straddled four-eyes slapping
cheeks rose in front of a cheerleader
who was too weak and popular to ask
him to stop. Her eyes marveled
at his desire to conquer. To gain

a father's praise, you try and fail
perfection, you obey without question,
but it's never enough:
you have to be a sacrifice.

He is no longer confused, no longer numb,
no longer a torturer, he weeps
for the strange love
between fathers and sons, for the genesis
of pain. Revelation has come to him
this afternoon while on the toilet taking
a shit tipping a dripping bottle to his lips.
He no longer fears a book whose spine is
broken.
He buckles looser, adds 2 inches
of rusty water to the bottle,
takes the first staggering steps
toward autonomy, declares *no,*
not dung to soldiers left for the carrion.

Fabricator, Pianist, Ventriloquist

A boy and a broken-wing sparrow,
their soaring moment on a trampoline.
Goooosh, a tardy lad and a father's
temper collide. The crying isn't
for the slap, but for a crush of joy.
Mother plates a casserole of smiles,
wears concealer for appearances,
disassociates from reality.

Months later, boy flutters to a girl
in a twirl of fancy obliterates
the truth, "I play the piano too,"
his head down, the worst ventriloquist
with a shirt pocket for a dummy.
She detects his pathetic lie and he
plays it off by flattery, a desperate
desire to please.

His fibs will be fabulously applied
far beyond self-conscious youth.
He will sail the Gulf of Tonkin,
play an abstract mime in Roma, see
another famous cousin die, swing
into the majors for his soaring lies.

The girl plays "Truth Divine" for him,
but he learns to lie by ear not heart.

No True Route

Merge or stop,
left or right,
departure or arrival-

you need directions
from strangers
for inward destinations too.

Marsh Deer

They pratfall a journey
between twisted shrub oaks,
part the blades of saw palmettos,
glide through the last dry tickle
of bristle grass and foxtail.

More like a string
of hooved prayer beads
giving thanks to the wilds,
Their resolve, moss-draped,
asks the dawn for its deepening,
stands under its roseamber wonder.

They tease the surf—
it greets them kissing
with wide smiles and quick legs.
They kick and circle
the white tailed mystery.

What draws them
to the white foam,
to the promise of crossings?
What makes any creature
choose uncertain currents?

Green turtle hatchlings,
bull sharks circling in creeks,
the bric-a-brac of shattered shells,
translucent dreams,
heart-shaped impressions
disappearing on a declivitous shore.

Lives are as fleeting as bird songs,
as long as letting go.

II

Ring of Fire

I.

Maybe for you it is a field
in Tuscany or Mexico or Kansas
but I am a shoeless child held
by a mother's smile in her tanned arms
and my grandfather leading us down
a tribal path across a rocky field
to behold for the first time—sunflowers
wild and multi-headed faces
hearing joy clapping they turn and watch
so began my sacred kinship
with a rangy and dangerous lot

II.

I prayed under their upswept stance
gorged on their seeds, delighted
in their crusty loaves, watched them
dominate fields, they have filled
my world with birds taught me
a thousand words for beauty.
Some are single-minded but bi-colored;
some have a mystery at the center
(some say dark but not me); bright
yellow or green or pale lemon or shaggy
but all sun blessed, sun kissed

III.

And each time I see the faces
of my woods-walking grandfather
and my sweet sun-kissed mother,
I wonder now who whispered to me
to grow, who told me to face east
to avoid the blaze and who it was
that taught me to face the inevitable
to refuse to lie
dormant in grief, to know
that better days will follow
when we witness the death
of a grandfather, a sweet mother,
and if we feel hardness coming
we don't stay encased in the husk
but spiral toward the golden angle
of the flower dazzled again
and again by the ring of fire
surrounding us.

The Felling

There are prophets not the ones
of words but of connectedness.
I met one who walks angel
oak branches, puts ear to trees;
hears pain and rot.
When he removes a shirt, you
see a waist and chest muscled from
chainsaws, tattooed with thrushes,
he climbs to the highest limbs,
strums to the wind. But

these gifts never come easy,
at twelve he's fetches his father
from bars but never makes it out.
Hears the bands howl and pick songs
but wood is what captivates
him, laminates their journey.
Mahogany and flame maple,
swamp ash and rosewood,
reverberate sweetness to him.
At forty, his father cut

from his life by fate with a
thousand old trees and branches.
Without his hearing aides, he's
gone deaf to voice except his

gut that stirs a hackberry
felling to safe direction
between roof and white cedar.
He shows me a photograph
of a 400-year-old live oak
limbs spread to an inversion

where candles are lit and drip wax,
composes songs on tonewood,
sits on the tailgate at dusk
truck crammed with dead limbs.
He will tell you the moment
before the branch is cut their leaves
change colors and trees tremble.
Once down, other limbs bend and
curl around the wound. He works
alone. Listens for their sounds.

Whispers of Trees

Slice out your tongue,
surrender your worries
when you are able,
escape your bonds,
enter the biome,
wind-swept pilgrim.

The trees whisper,
you are seeds of splintered light.
In a communion of roots,
our lives tremble

for an invitation
to connectedness.
We ponder
under a cathedral,
craning only for

perspective.
Measure yourself
by how a towering
moment passes.
Absorb the wafer
of woodland,
the fall of time.

Theology of Terrain

Inspired by the photography of Kathleen Robbins and Maude Schuyler Clay

I. Delta Dogs

Dogs in the delta
        howling a depth of field
in rows of spent cotton.
        Rambling, wailing travelers
sniffing the forgotten praise
        hymns of ruined field churches.
More like specks in ruts.
        the foreground, the background,

part of a theology of terrain,
        both genuflection to color
and black and white timelessness.
        Abandoned bridges, leaky barns,
rusted lives
of faithful and forgotten owners,
        different seasons where
same is not the same

yet a foregone conclusion.
        The delta brings them into
its depth across the mounds
        of the native dead.

Their four-legged scope
embraces the vastness
of sky and soil.

Moonlit howls across muddy gorges,
the virility of swamp hunts,
smells of the earth's
decay surround them.
Delta dogs greet the dead,
always ready to mark
a homemade headstone.

II. Turnrow

That sly thing had chased
          must a been a million
blackbirds from the bean field
          to the sky in a flapping fervent.
I was standing with Percy
          and the others near where
we hang the Christmas deer
          neither of us looking to the clouds.
This wasn't our first hunt.

When Percy saw the tail cross the turnrow,
          he let go a yelp of pleasing.
I knew we had'em almost skinned.
          Percy and the pack took off,
the music from their mouths
          impels chase across the field.

Waiting for Percy's got'em call,
          I went dead as a dry stalk.
My daddy, a childhood memory,
          an apparition in khaki shorts
with bare bow legs, white and rounded,
          standing in the skinning house
patting my bottom and saying
          this won't hurt a bit son.
Percy and the pack were closing in.

We would've caught that fox
        if I had stayed in the chase
just stayed in the chase
        but everything's now long gone—
the blackbirds, the dogs,
        the fox, the beans in the field,
nothing left but the turnrow.

It seemed like the distance
        was finally coming closer,
everything had gone to chase it here,
        the mystery of horizon, infinity's mask
beneath my feet all the time.

III. Cadillac

I caught the familiar sound
        its engine in the distance
tracking in the ruts for me
        with its flaky, faded paint
stained with the shit
        of a million geese
that never go home anymore.

Every Sunday of my youth,
        its hood ornament aligned
like a rifle sight
        on a cotton cross church.
Meanwhile deep in this land
        flows a vibrancy of promise.

When the window
        of the Cadillac fogged
I'd practice writing d-o-g
        my daddy would get tickled
at the awkwardly formed letters
        and say that's good son.
He would sit me on his lap
        and let me steer the ruts home,
tell me to watch for the pack
        coming outta the field.

IV. Percy

Percy, Percy is that you?
        You're music to my soul.
Damn boy I thought I'd lost you.
        Lift it up and let it go boy,
mark a good one, Percy.
        I got to tell you some things,
this delta is alive, alive again—

foxes in the kudzu tangle,
        trains in the depot,
barns purposed, bridges spanning, tractors
        sweeping, all of us in fields
harvesting the vibrant blues of living
        and the horizon, Percy,
you don't have to chase it anymore,
        wait on it to come to you, wait
like a man standing in a beanfield, Percy,
        shading his eyes to a vision,
dogs all upon the Delta.

Motion Detectors

Is there a safe path
even with a light aimed
perfectly on the walkway
or upon the camellia bushes?
We imagine a world
with shadows everywhere,
lurking to steal lives.
Each corner of the house
wired waiting to chase away
a two-legged rascal but usually
illuminating a rotund raccoon
on another garbage raid
or the neighbor's cat twitching its tail
on the roof of a Prius.
When the wind bends the branch
to jiggle in front of its lens,
we crack the door
to check—convinced we know
why it goes on and off.
We glower at them as they shine upon
what it is we fear,
the perils of living
with creatures like us.

III

Conventional Wisdom

Red-tailed hawks circle the city
ripping out the breast meat of
pigeons and backyard chickens,
black flies swarm to eyes over bridges,
pot holes and metal plates ruin tires
on main thoroughfares, expensive
lamps have been added by the upscale
condos, while older street lights stay
busted, one rests on the muddy bank
of the river like a beacon of warning,
smashed from its perch by a careening
SUV, broken glass and bits of metal collect
in bike lanes, battered 18 wheelers hauling
stacked cages release chicken feathers
that float up and spiral over fences,
thick foundation caulk has cracked in
downtown churches creating a mephitic
smell from spiritual bowels, cigarette butts
welcome the sick to hospital entrances,
tap water pours out brown, newspaper ads are
trapped in metal grates touting greener foods,
texting drivers pound horns turning onto
cell-to-ear pedestrians, decorative grasses
capture plastic bags from grocery stores,
wild geese have stopped to rest in river
currents and will stay due to the warming

weather conditions, cars are stained with the
shit of wild geese, homeless men pedal small-
frame bicycles facing traffic even though
conventional wisdom says this is a perilous
practice, they insist on seeing what's coming.

A History of Dirt

1. never too early

A robin cocks its head
to detect seismic murmurs,
the wild beating of your heart.

In this blessed life,
it's never too early
to risk —

every segment of yourself,
to rejoice in each moment
you cheat the robin's beak.

2. out of ovens

Bootstrapped, raped and swept
out of the ovens like dust
We survive despite wisdom
or faith on cursed ground.

We build a life upon it,
wipe our feet on bone.
In this dwelling of scars,
the history of dirt is blood.

3. wings

Dark wings rustle at the edge
of a meadow that's been
hewn, blasted, bled on,
and buried its share of bodies.
But there are still worms in its ground,
good inclinations that refuse to quit.
They burrow to make dirt wholly;
to purify, enrich, transform us.
They work in soiled silence,
deserve glory.

Hens and Chicks

In this squirrel of trouble,
turn to your inheritance,
the clippings of sisterhood,
grown in grief-watered soil, pap
for the driest times.

Poised on pickets in tins,
perched next to foundations,
on ledges in terracotta,
clustering in tight-lipped resolve,

Rallying to you again
and again, blooming, perishing,
a descendancy of tough rosettes,
the succulent hearts of kinswomen.

Caregiver

She doesn't pretend it's good,
there's nothing left for her to do.

The sheets remain bone dry,
lungs and heart are drowning.

Dying isn't supposed to make sense,
helplessness fills another morphine syringe.

Sing hymns but come the moment
nobody will bring hope-filled casseroles.

On a table, a photograph of them giggling,
born 1 ½ years, a mole, and insurance apart.

Pigeons peck the last seed she spread,
men in suits bounce the gurney down steps.

She pulls down the floral roll-up blinds,
phones her mother with dementia.

Aporia

A daughter spreads a mother's legs,
reveals a goddess on a PVC throne,
reveals a name eyes can no longer say.
In the clearing aporia of a morning shower,
the background tune, "Whenever you call me
I'll be there." Mother and daughter shop
together on Saturdays take item upon item to
their ineffable dimension. In a ballet of
appraisal, swearing their husbands would
transform, transform, in button-down sweater
vests. Socratically questioning if purple
umbrella stands blend in landlocked cottage-
style homes. Pleading, pleading for the other
to buy something, anything, while moving in a
corps de ballet with adagio steps to the next
aisle until there are no more aisles to glide
down together. A life reduced to the vagaries
of a fondue blueprint, black and white subway
tile in fresh thin set, a floor engineered so that
the water flows to a central drain, forcing
everything down pipes, pipes. The accessible
shower, a mother, a daughter, the overstated
floral print of a shower curtain, galaxies past
cottage-style, an early warning ignored but
now enough to wake them from a spell, to

complete her dressing in pink and brown. She
spreads the moisturizer on her mother's
cheek, making sure she gets the dry spot near
the nose, dabs her same dry spot.

Ode to a **M**ender

She spends a life on
the threads of doing
one task after another.
Flat sure as an iron
straightening out
more than wrinkles.
Ignores desires
like a meddling fool.
Understands herself,
wants to mend torn cloth.
Crease after crease, gathers,
folds the fabric closer.

Rare Flowers

Consider the lilies of the field—

they better be perfect, fragrant,
how we want them
never toiling nor spinning.

But there are rare flowers, arrayed
with frailty, like children
imperfect and wild,
luminaries, never picked,
most precious.

Llama

a child whisked
to his first circus
of concentric visions

the clown tumbles
operatically the anthem
riding on an elephant

his hand rises upward
to caress his father's cheek
he cries out "I love it"

fleeting is perfect
on the faces of his parents
the procession triumphs

he recognizes many animals
but grows transfixed
with the llama

they try to distract him
act upon act follows
he wants only the llama

it does not appear
until the end in a minor role
for him and no one else

Checkers

Sean, a violent boy, tells his therapist, Martha
that he pulls wings off angels and moths.
He scans, scans the room for them
but instead spots the red-top in the corner.
Martha suggests, "Let's play checkers."

A shy chatter about his father begins,
of music, of pauses, of measured beatings.
He recalls screaming, "har-der fuck-er,"
to a song in the background.
Martha smells fresh skid marks.

Between sessions, he smashes windshields
considers moves, returns with misdirection;
Martha unleashes a double jump.
Sean shits a checker-sized turd, fidgets
shouts, "you-moth-er-fuc-ker," to the game.

Between sessions, he fights faces and faces
of his father on street corners until his
knuckles are crimson and smudged pieces.
There's no denying a desire to be loved
or the blockade trapping him on a diagonal.

In a breakthrough session, he hums the song.
Martha mouths, "Un-for-gett-a-ble."
"It is," sobs Sean. He shreds the board
hurls plastic, plastic fucking men to the
ground.
Martha tells him he's a boy with wings.

Riddle

It raises questions.
It wants to be held.
A child's might seek ears.
How many times does it wipe away tears?
How often does it break?
It feels the smallest crucifixions
and tangles love.
Toss it up because you understand nothing.
Each bone, each space,
a feral voice, and a keening silence,
let it rest on the hip of another.
Its touch—communicable.
They'll put a gun in it,
force it to finger your neighbor,
"the perfect suspect" in the geopolitical state.
A kite of flesh to fly around the body.

IV

Prison

We build our own prisons. Maybe
you didn't get the job offer
or the acceptance letter.

Maybe you tell fibs
to feel better until
a door's nailed shut. Soon

slights are magnified
by guards whispering
you've been made a fool of

by a stepfather who pours
imports for guests while you
get domestic. A plainclothes

truth follows; you've made
a jailhouse bed. There is
inmate snitching because

you drank too much or ate
cake late at night.
You pace until you forget

there was ever unfenced
laughter or pubs full
of friends waiting. One lifer

chips through walls, crawls,
escapes shadows, and scales
fences for a Lab to slobber

a face with perspective.
For some, agonizing heartbreak
will make walls fall.

Drinks Purposely

Inspired by "I Am Sapelo," Cornelia Walker Bailey's account of Sapelo, Georgia.

A free man hunts squirrels and possums,
          drinks moonshine purposely,
loves to tell stories.

Stares buzzards off the ground,
          keeps an ear for shotgun blasts,
sleeps on the ground of what's coming.

Snatches a stomach of a hog
          pounds it thin in smoldering ash,
blows a balloon for children.

Spits while crossing big water,
          hums Gullah air, Gullah air
          to dead slaves of tidal creeks,
steers his boat with flaring sides.

Apertures

In a soft composition of rain,
then an outpouring of grand expanse,
rising to the hackberry, overwhelming
the new deck, we fled a thousand years.

When floodwaters recede, the flesh of homes
sullied and sick, we focus lenses to memories,
cross thresholds as shadow and light. See
the demarcation of chance, watermarks

on walls above the ruin of below.
Bone dry oystermen in Savannah,
wet muck on fresh-in-love faces,
emulsion peeling layers of occasion

from photos not worth another word.
Toss albums into dumpsters,
curse cameras from unlivable spaces,
their apertures fixed to fate.

Was it ever real? Our trip to Italy?
The wedding on the beach at Edisto?
Stubbornly adhering to each other,
no longer salvageable.

Blessed

1. Eye-lined

Hair frosted in a wooden pew,
wrenching and kneeling—
a pocketbook of judgment
dressed in the latest salvation.
Wearing Anne Klein for Jesus,
even the preacher eye-lined.
Everyone singing to the choir
in a cathedral of glances;
you need the unison amen.
In this house, success is a symbol
of what God can do.
The blessed repeat their prayer for the poor.
Thank God, it is not me.

2. Immaculate Consumption

You avoid the fancy coffee line
and bless Jen for a simple cup.
A smooth varietal and a chosen booth—
everything is vital about this ritual.
You bow thanks to a reverent flavor.
The world closed from the inside,
meanwhile these grounds bear witness
to resurrections one sip at a time.

The Last Figure Eights

One more story of the Gulfstream
swells until the barnacled
bottoms of tankers are roofs. Let
others stand on bridges
to watch the parade go by. Old
sailors untie figure eights
from docks, hoist sails,
navigate through wreckage.
They guzzle memories, drain
the last drop, and slip infinity
from cleats. Let salt eat the varnish
until the teak is bare.
Steer voyages with stars.
Reclaim the stolen wind.

A Tidal River Answers Prayer

Pat Conroy (1945-2016), for Cassandra

I.

Dear Tidal River, immerse me
in the world below bridges.
Mud my youth within you,
poultice a desperate need
away from the roaring of
fighter pilots at tables,
away from backhanded love.
Soak away family secrets
and heal my unseen bruises.

Submerge me in stories
through a thousand eyes and mouths.
Lead me to curvatures of
remarkable passage,
to salute awe-soaked fiddlers,
to marvel at the courtship of herons.
Dare me to leap off docks,
to hear your rhythmic songs,
to feel the ooze of pluff between my toes
and sink into creation.

Teach me to listen to your call,
the beckoning of tides.

II.

Hear my prayer, Tidal River,
call me at the hour of my tide.
Incantations lift sea foam
in prisms of light like sunrise.

But sunrise will not come for me.

Oh, Osprey! Winged messenger!
Skim my soul across the river,
slip it soundless in the tide.
I leave to write alone, our lives
but water slipping to the sea.

Already it is turning.
I watch a world from my back,
my neck cranes with excitement.
Eyes of turtles, conchs, ghost crabs,
bull sharks bump against
my thigh to remind me it's
precious to be alive.
Devilfish stir in the sound
darken pinpricks of starlight
through the murk of no longer.
I swim soft body to a shell
abandoned in Battery Creek.

III.

Generous River let others
find currents of conviction
to write what must be written.

Drink, love, live:
all in good company,
this a shimmering body.
Swim the storied river,
occupy a geography,
with gonads for the truth.

For this River rescues,
crosses us to shores
reveals the stories we must tell,
answer tides with words,
Amen.

Immortal

Death whether seen or unseen,
doesn't manifest a direction,
nor lurk on the periphery,
but stirs in us with the first wail of a child.

Is it the cry you hear when you die?
Whether it is or not, we die immortal
on ordinary days filled with wonder
gathering and passing through.

The Best Part

The truth be known,
gay or straight,

the priest gets paid,
the nun has a shitty deal,
the minister wants his ass kissed.

Meanwhile I have felt a voice
in the forest of owls and ordinary spaces.
Strangers have rescued me from peril;
like you, love has saved me.

Your neighbor is human.
We don't listen or tell it right,
we take it literally,
we can't write it down better,
we make it too complicated.

Who have you loved in this journey?
What is it you have given?

Acknowledgements

To the perfect editor, the gifted poet, Ed Madden who guided me with kindness and precision through this project. To the strength, grace, and talent of Cassandra King. To Marjory Wentworth, Poet Laureate of South Carolina who encouraged me to find my poems. To Kathleen Robbins for allowing me to use the photo "Blackbirds" from her incredible book of photography *Into the Flatland* on the cover. To all who support the vital role of small publishing houses like Muddy Ford Press, and to Cindi Boiter and Bob Jolley for their passion to publish emerging writers and poets.

Greatest love and honor to my siblings and their spouses; Carol (who lit the flame), Mike and Jean, Kathy and Bobbie, Jim and Janice, and the beloved departed; our parents, Don and Peg, and brothers, Pat and Tom. And to the family that stretches love across time; Jessica, Bill, Elise, and Stella; Melissa, Jay, Wester, and Lila; Megan, Mollie, Jack, and Katie; Rachel, Andy, and Henry; Michael; and Willie and Laura. To Barbara Conroy for helping this teenage boy in 1974.

To the memory of Sam Morton who invited me to join *Ink Plots*, a supportive tribe of writers. To John Tatara for our many near death hiking adventures. To Mitchel Yell for chess and optimism. To Ellen Malphrus and Andy Fishkind for the comfort they bestowed. To Ray McManus, John Harper, Janice Owens, Rebekah Maxwell, and Catherine Seltzer for tolerating random emails. To friendships at Needle Acres with Michael Miller and Anita and Geoffrey Graves. To the companions, sunsets, and smoked wings at Bar None. To my incredible neighbors the Pinewood Friends.

To talks about the work with Al Black, Carla Damron, Ethan Fogus, and Curtis Derrick. To Amy, Scott, and Alan Basnett for anchorage and shared grief. To Dr. Dufford for fighting for worthy causes. To the esoteric knowledge and friendship of Jonathan Hanna and Maggie Schein. To Martha and Bernie Schein for their insights on teaching and healing. To Jonathan Haupt for leading the Pat Conroy Literary Center, and to his insightful wife, Lorene for putting up with us all. To the Board members, Maura Connelly, and the ambassadors at the Conroy Center who make the effort possible. To all educators, especially those I witnessed in action at Pine Grove School, Sandel, Browns Ferry, and Andrews Elementary. To rescuers and caregivers. To those who seek conviction.

Notes

"A Tidal River Answers Prayer" is for Cassandra.

"A Wrath of Verses" is for John Harper.

"Apertures" is for Kathleen Robbins.

"Assurances" is for Colonel Donald Conroy (RIP).

"Checkers" is for Martha Schein.

"Fabricator, Pianist, Ventriloquist" is for Amy Basnett.

"Hens and Chicks", "Caregiver", "Aporia" and "Mender" are for Terrye, Deborah (RIP), and Jerrye.

"Llama" is for Jackson Weathers.

"Rare Flowers" is for Tristan and Delilah Bonnert.

"Ring of Fire" is for Margaret Peek Conroy Egan (RIP) and Jasper Peek (RIP).

"The Last Figure Eights" is for Andy Fishkind and Ross Basnett (RIP).

"Two Little Joes" is for Thomas Patrick Conroy (RIP).

"Whisper of Trees" is for John Tatara, a.k.a. "Peter Pan," an AT thru-hiker 94 and 97, volunteer, and trail maintainer.

There is a "Theology of Terrain" video, produced and directed by Drew Baron, as part of Kathleen Robbins' installation of "Descent: Mississippi Delta photographs 1999–2014" at the Columbia Museum of Art. (2016).

https://www.columbiamuseum.org/cma_stories/theology-terrain-tim-conroy

Editor Acknowledgments

My grateful acknowledgement is given to the editors of the following publications where these poems first appeared.

"Apertures" appeared in *Marked by the Water: Artists Respond to a Thousand Year Flood.* Muddy Ford Press. (2016).

A version of "Theology of Terrain" appeared in *Fall Lines: a literary convergence* Volume III (2016).

A version of "Llama" appeared in *Fall Lines: a literary convergence* Volume II. (2015)

A version of "Immaculate Consumption," (Coffee House) appeared in a collection of poetry for the Comet, Columbia's bus system, selected by Ed Madden, Poet Laureate for city of Columbia. (2015).

About the Cover Artist

Kathleen Robbins is professor of art, coordinator of the photography program, and affiliate faculty of southern studies at the University of South Carolina. Born in Washington DC and raised in the Mississippi Delta, Robbins received her MFA from the University of New Mexico. Her photographs have been exhibited in galleries and museums including The Halsey Museum of Contemporary Art, The New Orleans Photo Alliance, Virginia MOCA, The Light Factory Museum of Contemporary Photography & Film, The Weatherspoon Museum, John Michael Kohler Art Center, the Ogden Museum of Southern Art, Addison Gallery of American Art, The Southeast Museum of Photography, the Society for Contemporary Photography, and the Mississippi Museum of Art. Robbins' work has also been featured by CNN Photo Blog, *Flak Photo*, *Fraction Magazine*, Conscientious, Humble Arts New York, NPR's Picture Show, PDN's Photo of the Day, *Oxford American*, and *Garden and Gun*. In 2012, she was part of the Critical Mass top 50 and she was the recipient of the 2011 PhotoNOLA Review Prize. A limited edition book of *Into the Flatland* was published by the New Orleans Photo Alliance in 2012. A monograph of *Into the Flatland* was published by the USC Press in 2015.

About the Author

Tim Conroy is a former special education teacher, school administrator, and vice president of the South Carolina Autism Society. His poetry and short fiction have been published in literary journals, magazines, and compilations, including *Fall Lines*, *Auntie Bellum*, and *Marked by the Water*. A founding board member of the Pat Conroy Literary Center, established in his brother's honor, Conroy lives and writes in Columbia, South Carolina.

CPSIA information can be obtained
at www.ICGtesting.com
Printed in the USA
LVOW13s0918280118
564316LV00041B/1053/P